APR 22

FACT AND FICTION OF AMERICAN HISTORY

FACT AND FICTION OF AMERICAN INVENTION

BY TAMMY GAGNE
CONTENT CONSULTANT
Paul Israel, PhD
Research Professor and Director of the Thomas A. Edison Papers Project
Rutgers University

Core Library

An Imprint of Abdo Publishing
abdobooks.com

Cover image: Thomas Edison began inventing in his 20s and continued into his 80s.

abdobooks.com

Published by Abdo Publishing, a division of ABDO, PO Box 398166, Minneapolis, Minnesota 55439. Copyright © 2022 by Abdo Consulting Group, Inc. International copyrights reserved in all countries. No part of this book may be reproduced in any form without written permission from the publisher. Core Library™ is a trademark and logo of Abdo Publishing.

Printed in the United States of America, North Mankato, Minnesota
052021
092021

THIS BOOK CONTAINS RECYCLED MATERIALS

Cover Photo: Library of Congress, colorized by Mighty Media Press
Interior Photos: Bettmann/Getty Images, 4–5, 20–21; PF-(usna)/Alamy , 7; Shutterstock Images, 9, 34 (top); Everett Collection Historical/Alamy, 12–13; Everett Historical/Shutterstock Images, 15, 18, 26–27 (bottom right), 45; Hemin Xylan/Shutterstock Images, 17; Morphart Creation/Shutterstock Images, 22; Library of Congress, colorized by Mighty Media Press, 26 (top left), 26 (top right); Library of Congress, 29 (top); Science & Society Picture Library/SPPL/Getty Images, 29 (bottom); Ullstein Bild/Getty Images, 32, 43; United States Patent and Trademark Office, 34 (bottom); agefotostock/Alamy, 39

Editor: Aubrey Zalewski
Series Designer: Ryan Gale

Library of Congress Control Number: 2020948280

Publisher's Cataloging-in-Publication Data

Names: Gagne, Tammy, author.
Title: Fact and fiction of American invention / by Tammy Gagne
Description: Minneapolis, Minnesota : Abdo Publishing, 2022 | Series: Fact and fiction of American history | Includes online resources and index.
Identifiers: ISBN 9781532195099 (lib. bdg.) | ISBN 9781098215408 (ebook)
Subjects: LCSH: Inventions--United States--History--Juvenile literature. | Technology--Juvenile literature. | Truthfulness and falsehood--Juvenile literature. | Public opinion--Juvenile literature.
Classification: DDC 670--dc23

CONTENTS

CHAPTER ONE
Who Thought of It First? 4

CHAPTER TWO
Taking All the Credit 12

CHAPTER THREE
Bright Ideas 20

CHAPTER FOUR
Going Places 26

CHAPTER FIVE
Overlooked 34

Important Dates 42

Stop and Think 44

Glossary 46

Online Resources 47

Learn More 47

Index 48

About the Author 48

CHAPTER ONE

WHO THOUGHT OF IT FIRST?

The popular board game Monopoly has been around for decades. Players rush to buy up as much property as possible. Then they charge rent to other players who land on each property. One popular story about Monopoly's invention says that the idea for the game came from a man named Charles Darrow. He had the idea while unemployed. Many people assumed that Darrow was dreaming of financial success. But today people know more about the story.

Charles Darrow retired as a millionaire one year after selling Monopoly to Parker Brothers.

PERSPECTIVES

DEFENDING AN IDEA

In 1868, Margaret Knight invented a machine that would give paper bags flat bottoms. Then they would not tip over. A man named Charles Annan tried to steal Knight's idea. He filed a patent for the invention. But Knight sued him and won. She went on to file more than 20 patents in her lifetime. Ryan P. Smith wrote an article for *Smithsonian Magazine* about Knight's fight for recognition. In it he said, "No doubt many female inventors of the early 1900s—and later—were spurred on by Knight's courageous example."

In 1934, Darrow sent his idea for the game to Parker Brothers. This company was a successful toy company. It bought the rights to Monopoly from Darrow in 1935. But the company also paid a woman named Elizabeth Magie. She had patented a remarkably similar game in 1904. She called her invention the Landlord's Game.

Magie thought that monopolies were bad for society. If a few people owned too much real estate, they could charge an unreasonable amount of rent. She created her game

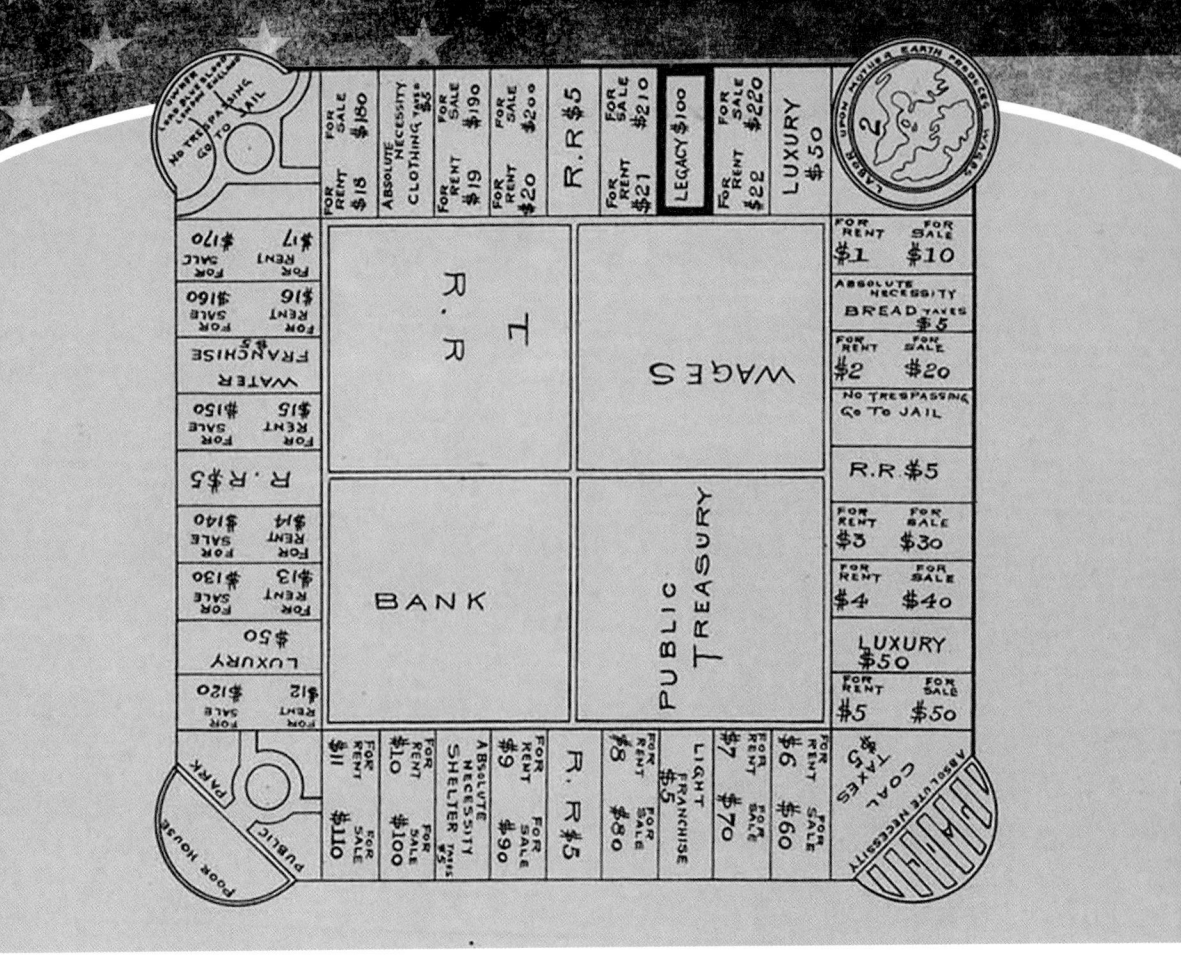

Elizabeth Magie may have spent more money creating and patenting the Landlord's Game than she earned from it.

to point out that monopolies take away competition. Competition keeps costs reasonable. Magie's game taught this with two sets of rules. One was against monopolies and one was for them. Magie played the Landlord's Game with her family and friends. They then shared it with others. The game spread.

Darrow learned of the Landlord's Game in 1932 while he was unemployed. He used the set of rules that had monopolies as the goal. Darrow based his game on that version. The goal was to own as many properties as possible. One by one, players would run out of money. The last person standing was the winner.

Although Darrow changed the names of the streets, the basic board layout matched Magie's game. He even left the spaces she called "Chance" and "Jail" on his own board. But Darrow

> **HAPPY ACCIDENTS**
>
> Some inventors create things by accident. Charles Goodyear is a prime example. Goodyear spent years trying to make a type of rubber that would not crack in the heat or cold. In 1839, he left a batch of rubber and sulfur on a hot stove by mistake. The heat and sulfur made rubber durable. This accident led to the creation of pencil erasers, rubber balls, and automobile tires.

Darrow's first Monopoly board was circular. Later it was sold as a square.

made millions on the deal with Parker Brothers. Magie walked away with just $500.

WHEN FICTION OVERSHADOWS FACT

Inventions begin with the design of a new product or process. Many invention stories center on a single person. This is usually the person who put the finishing touches on an invention or who made it popular. Many stories about a single inventor are incomplete. Most inventions rely on the work of many people. Each person provides another step toward the final product. Inventors build on each other's ideas. Sometimes they even work on the same idea at the same time. Some inventors are overlooked because of their gender, race, or class. A story of a famous inventor can be exciting to hear and retell. But it often isn't the whole story.

STRAIGHT TO THE
SOURCE

Sarah Koch works at the Case Foundation. The Case Foundation supports entrepreneurship and invention. In a post to the foundation's blog, Koch discusses how truthful invention stories can inspire future inventors.

> *The history and the future of entrepreneurship are full of interesting and diverse characters and stories of great teamwork—and much more interesting than the myths and the models that continue to dominate the narrative. The most powerful ideas are really borne out of a "village," more than they are happened upon in a rare "aha moment" by a single entrepreneur. . . . Changing that narrative to better reflect reality has the potential to actually make it a reality for more people, in more places, from more backgrounds.*

Source: Sarah Koch. "The Myth of Isolation." *Case Foundation*, 24 Nov. 2015, casefoundation.org. Accessed 15 June 2020.

CONSIDER YOUR AUDIENCE

Adapt this passage for a different audience, such as your friends. Write your own blog post conveying this same information for the new audience. How does your post differ from the original text and why?

CHAPTER
TWO

TAKING ALL THE CREDIT

Most inventors want credit for their successful ideas and hard work. But many stories overlook the people who made advances toward an invention. For example, Elisha Otis takes credit for inventing the passenger elevator. But similar lifting devices had been around for hundreds of years. During this time, elevators were not reliable. The materials often broke. When this happened, the elevators fell. This made elevators risky for human use.

Otis added a critical feature. In 1852, Otis built a device to keep elevators from falling

Elisha Otis demonstrated his safety hoist at the New York World's Fair in 1854.

if ropes gave out. He named it the safety hoist. This device made elevators much more dependable. And elevators still use it today.

Otis was not the only person to solve this problem. In 1859, Otis Tufts patented a screw mechanism that also made elevators safer. But Tufts's design was more complicated and expensive. It was not as successful, and Elisha Otis was the inventor who went down in history.

ESSENTIAL TO MODERN CONSTRUCTION

The designers of New York City's Chrysler Building and Empire State Building used elevators. These were equipped with Elisha Otis's safety hoist. The hoist was also used in the construction of the Eiffel Tower in Paris. Without Otis's device, skyscrapers might not exist today. Riding an elevator with no safety device to the tops of these tall buildings would be very dangerous.

THE TYPEWRITER

Many say that Christopher Latham Sholes invented the typewriter. After years of working on it, Sholes

Christopher Latham Sholes's daughter Lillian demonstrated an early version of his typewriter in 1872.

put his typewriter on the market in 1874. This machine helped people type large amounts of text. But Sholes wasn't the only one who made such a device. More than 50 other inventors had created similar machines. William Burt built the first known typewriter in 1830.

Early typewriters arranged the letters in the order of the alphabet. This made the keys easy to find. But it also caused problems. One problem was that typewriters often jammed. This occurred when a person struck letters that were next to each other. Many words contained these combinations of letters. Sholes fixed this problem. He changed the layout of the letters. He created the QWERTY keyboard. It was named for the first six letters on the top row of keys. Computer keyboards still use this layout.

Sholes wasn't the only person who worked on his typewriter. Fellow inventors Carlos Glidden and Samuel W. Soulé helped him. Once the inventors had a reliable model, the company E. Remington and Sons

PERSPECTIVES
WAS THAT REALLY THE REASON?

Some people challenge whether the QWERTY keyboard was designed to keep common letter pairings separate. If this was the plan for the design, Sholes did not arrange the letters perfectly. Jimmy Stamp is a writer for *Smithsonian Magazine*. He points out, "This theory could be easily debunked for the simple reason that 'er' is the fourth most common letter pairing in the English language." It does seem that Sholes was aware of the "er" issue. Early versions of his design replaced the letter *r* with the period key. But his later patented design placed the two letters side by side.

Modern keyboards on computers and smartphones still use Sholes's QWERTY layout.

promoted it. The support of the company helped the QWERTY typewriter become popular.

THE TELEPHONE

Alexander Graham Bell is famous for inventing the telephone in 1876. That was the year he received

The device Alexander Graham Bell used to make the first phone call looked very different from telephones today.

the patent for it. Bell was indeed part of the invention's story. But he was not the sole inventor of the device. Both Bell and another man named Elisha Gray worked on different telephones. They finished their projects around the same time. It came down to who could file a patent first. They both filed patent paperwork on the same day.

When Bell received the patent, Gray filed a lawsuit. The courts kept the patent with Bell because his lawyer had made it to the patent office before Gray's. Bell got all the credit. But many historians still question who deserved the credit. Some say that Bell's model was at least partly based on Gray's design.

EXPLORE ONLINE

Chapter Two discusses the invention of the typewriter. The website below includes information about the typewriter. As you know, every source is different. How is the information from the website the same as the information in Chapter Two? What new information did you learn from the website?

A BRIEF HISTORY OF TYPEWRITERS

abdocorelibrary.com/fact-fiction-american-invention

CHAPTER THREE

BRIGHT IDEAS

Thomas Edison has gone down in history as one of the most famous American inventors. During his lifetime, he held 1,093 different patents. This is more than any other inventor. Edison is best known for inventing the light bulb in 1879. Stories about Edison and his famous bulb make it seem like he was the main inventor. In reality, other inventors had been working on this kind of project for many years. An inventor named Joseph Swan was working on a light bulb at the same time as Edison.

Thomas Edison built his light bulb in his laboratory in Menlo Park, New Jersey.

EDISON'S LIGHT BULB

Edison created a type of light bulb called an incandescent light bulb. In this type of bulb, electricity travels through one contact wire and reaches the filament. The filament gets so hot that it glows. The electricity flows out through the other contact wire. Edison used carbon filaments. Later, tungsten metal filaments became more popular. Edison's bulb had a vacuum that protected the filament. Later, bulbs were filled with gases. How does knowing this and seeing the different parts of Edison's light bulb help you understand why inventions often take many attempts?

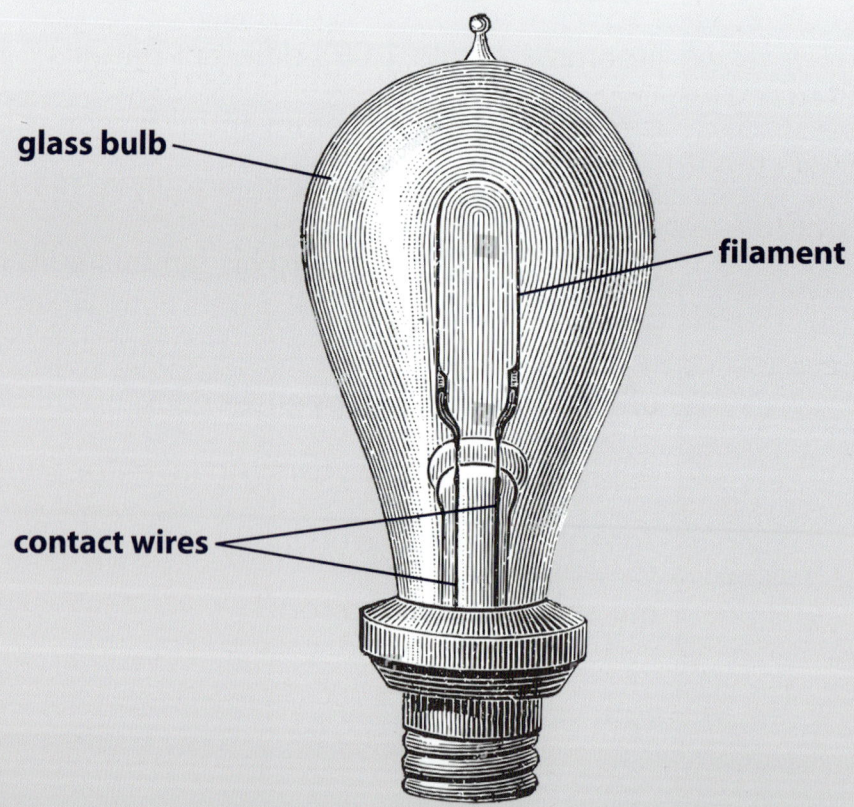

glass bulb

filament

contact wires

Before Edison, light bulbs were not very efficient. Inventors had run into problems with them. Some bulbs were too bright. They burned out too quickly. Others were very expensive to make. Edison made a bulb with a thin filament. He used a certain type of bamboo, which he turned into carbon. It produced just the right amount of light. It lasted for long periods of time. It also wasn't too expensive to make. All this made it possible for him to start making and selling an efficient bulb. He had his own laboratory and designed his bulb as part of an entire

PERSPECTIVES

EDISON THE MURDERER?

Myths about Edison include some shocking tales. One is that he killed one of his assistants. According to this story, Edison murdered Clarence Dally by exposing him to dangerous energy called X-rays. Biographer Paul Israel disputes this myth. "To say that Edison killed Dally is just nonsense," he insists. He goes on to explain that Dally did die from X-rays. But it wasn't Edison's fault. Many people who experimented with X-rays had health problems as a result.

WORKING FOR EDISON

Nikola Tesla briefly worked for Edison before branching out on his own. In 1881, Edison founded a manufacturing company called Edison Machine Works. It produced generators for his famous electrical system. A list of the company's employees shows that Tesla was employed there. However, he did not work with Edison personally. He worked as an electrical engineer for about six months. Then he left to work on a different lighting system.

electrical system. Because of this, he became known as the inventor.

AC CURRENT

In the 1880s, many new inventions depended on electricity. Inventors raced to figure out the best way to get electricity to many people at once.

One of Edison's biggest rivals was an inventor named Nikola Tesla. Both men worked with electric currents. Edison worked with direct current (DC). In DC, electricity flows in a single direction. Tesla worked with alternating current (AC). This current can reverse the direction of electricity. Each inventor wanted his system to become the standard. In the end, Tesla's AC system was the more popular choice. It could be used over greater distances.

Tesla also was not the sole inventor of AC. An Italian inventor named Galileo Ferraris worked on an AC system around the same time as Tesla. Inventors Friedrich Haselwander, Charles Bradley, William Stanley, and Elihu Thomson focused their work on this goal as well. Tesla's contributions undoubtedly helped make AC the preferred system. But stories that give him all the credit are based more in fiction than fact.

FURTHER EVIDENCE

Chapter Three discusses Thomas Edison and his work developing the light bulb. What was one of the main points of this chapter? What evidence is included to support this point? Read the article at the website below. Does the information on the website support the main point of the chapter? Does it present new evidence?

THE HISTORY OF THE LIGHT BULB

abdocorelibrary.com/fact-fiction-american-invention

CHAPTER FOUR

GOING PLACES

The airplane was one of the greatest inventions of the 1900s. American brothers Orville and Wilbur Wright invented the airplane that made the first flight in 1903. Before airplanes, people relied on trains and ships for long-distance journeys. The trips could take days, weeks, or even months. Airplanes made it possible for people to travel all over the world in hours.

THE AIRPLANE

The Wright brothers' flight of the first airplane is one of the most amazing invention stories of

After their first flight, Orville Wright, *left*, and Wilbur Wright, *right*, continued to improve their airplane design.

PERSPECTIVES
HARD TO BELIEVE

When Orville and Wilbur Wright first invented their plane, not everyone believed it had actually flown. When the Wrights offered to sell their plane to the US government, the answer was no. The French government was interested. But many people questioned whether the story about the brothers' flight was true. An article published in a French newspaper read, "The Wrights have flown or they have not flown. They possess a machine or they do not possess one. They are in fact either fliers or liars."

all time. On December 17, 1903, the plane made its historic flight in Kitty Hawk, North Carolina. But it may not have been the first flight of its kind.

A 1901 article in Connecticut's *Bridgeport Sunday Herald* gave credit to Gustave Whitehead for the first-ever flight. The newspaper reported that his flight took place on August 14, 1901, in Fairfield, Connecticut. The article stated that Whitehead's plane flew up to 50 feet (15 m) in the air for a distance of approximately 2,640 feet (800 m). This is short

DIFFERENT
AIRPLANES

The airplanes of the Wright brothers and Whitehead looked very different from each other. What are some of the two airplanes' differences, based on the images below? What do differences suggest about the inventing process?

Whitehead's airplane, 1901

Wright brothers' airplane, 1903

compared to today's flights. But it was more than enough to classify the trip as the first flight. The Wright brothers' plane flew only 540 feet (165 m) during its famous flight.

But the *Bridgeport Sunday Herald* article may not have been true. The article was tucked away on the fifth page of the paper. And the flight was never repeated. Historians have said that one of the two witnesses later denied that the flight took place. Other witnesses came forward and said they had seen Whitehead's flight. But for now, the evidence is lacking about what really took place that day. Historians know Whitehead was working on an airplane. What is unclear is whether it actually flew.

Whitehead's plane may never have left the ground. But he did contribute to the invention of the airplane. His research was a step forward in airplane design. Inventions are accomplishments with many different steps. One person can rarely take all the credit.

THE AUTOMOBILE

Another inventor who made travel more efficient was Henry Ford. Ford's name appears in a blue oval logo on millions of automobiles sold each year. Many people think this famous auto maker invented the automobile in 1896. But as with so many other inventions, there is far more to this story.

Étienne Lenoir of France was among the first inventors to build an automobile. In 1862, Lenoir built the first automobile with an internal combustion engine. In 1864, German-Austrian inventor Siegfried Marcus also created his own version of the automobile. Later, in 1885, German inventor

> ## THE MYTH OF THE MODEL T
> Even Ford's own vehicles are the subjects of a myth or two. When many people think of Ford's first automobile, they picture the Model T. This early Ford automobile was indeed the first mass-produced vehicle. But the first automobile Ford made was the Quadricycle. It had no steering wheel or brake. It could not move in reverse.

With the moving assembly line, it only took 93 minutes to build a car. Before, it took approximately 12 hours.

Karl Benz created his first automobile. Today the car company Mercedes-Benz bears his name.

It is unclear how much each inventor knew of the others' designs. But the one thing that is certain is that no one person created an automobile completely on his or her own. The car was far too complicated for just one person to invent.

One reason Ford gets credit for inventing the automobile is that he perfected another invention that changed the world. That invention was the moving assembly line. This was an efficient arrangement of workers and machines in a factory. Each person in the line focused on one small part of the job. The assembly line made it possible to build a lot of automobiles in a short time. Ford began using the assembly line to mass-produce his automobiles in 1913. His cars were among the first to be sold to a large number of customers. Ford may not have invented the car. But he was the one to bring the invention to the public.

(No Model.)

J. L. LOVE.

PENCIL SHARPENER.

No. 594,114. Patented Nov. 23, 1897.

FIG. 1.

FIG. 2.

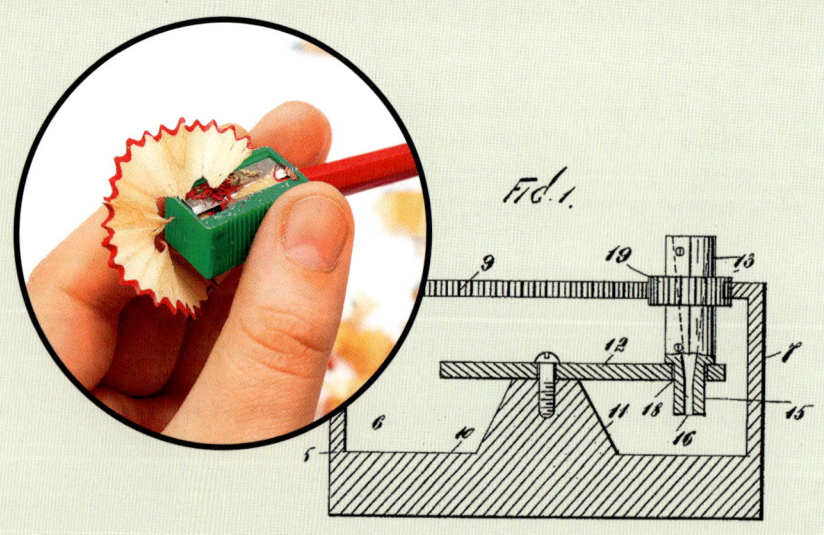

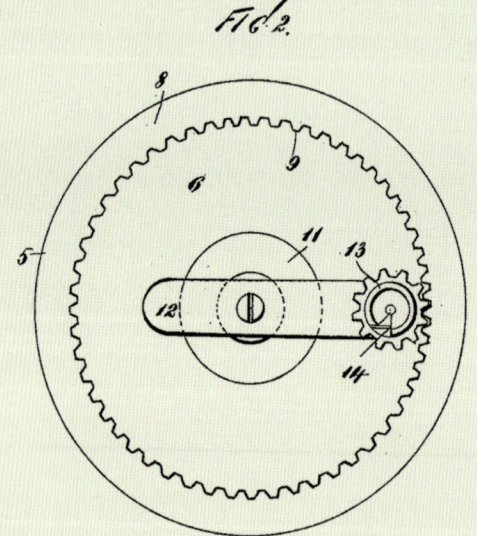

WITNESSES:

John Buckler,

C. Gerst.

INVENTOR

John Lee Love.

BY

Edgar Tate & Co

ATTORNEYS.

THE NORRIS PETERS CO., PHOTO-LITHO., WASHINGTON, D. C.

CHAPTER FIVE

OVERLOOKED

Made-up or exaggerated stories about who invented what may not seem like a big issue. But people who are forgotten in the retelling of invention stories were sometimes left out on purpose. Many forgotten inventors were women or people of color.

Nearly everyone knows the names of Henry Ford and Thomas Edison. But few know the story of John Lee Love. And many people use his invention regularly. Love was a Black carpenter in Fall River, Massachusetts, in the 1890s. Like most carpenters, he used

A handheld pencil sharpener is similar to John Lee Love's design with a cone-shaped hole and single blade.

> ## NO CREDIT
> In the 1850s, a Black man named Benjamin Montgomery invented a steamboat propeller. It could be used in the shallow waters of Mississippi State's waterways. It helped steamboats deliver food in the region. Although Montgomery applied for a patent, it was rejected because he was enslaved. Montgomery became a free man after the Civil War (1861–1865). Later, Montgomery became one of the largest cotton producers in the state.

a pencil to mark his measurements. At the time, pencil sharpeners were large and inconvenient. They used many blades to shave the pencil.

Love thought of a way to make the process better. In 1897, he designed a portable sharpener. It was a round chamber. At the center of the device was a short arm. The end of the arm had a hole shaped like a cone with a single blade. The user pushed the pencil into the hole at the end of the arm. The pencil was sharpened as the person rotated the arm around the chamber. The chamber held the shavings until the user emptied it.

Many people continue to use his basic design today. But Love's story has been overlooked because he was Black. Some people did not want to give invention credit to people of color.

THE WINDSHIELD WIPER

Sometimes small inventions make life much easier. Early automobiles did not come with windshield wipers. When it rained or snowed, drivers had to stop their cars, get out, and clear the windshields themselves. This extra step made every trip in bad weather take much longer. It could also be dangerous to pull over in rain or snow. A woman from Alabama changed the way people drove in the rain by inventing windshield wipers.

Mary Anderson was visiting New York City when the idea came to her. She was riding in a streetcar during a snowstorm. She waited for the driver to clear the windshield repeatedly. She thought how much time and effort someone could save if a device could do this work instead.

She came up with a new invention. Drivers could attach her device to a car during poor weather. They just needed to turn a handle to clear the windshield as needed. It could then be removed for driving on dry days. She called her invention the Window Cleaning Device. She patented it in 1903.

She tried to sell her invention to manufacturers. But they told her that the idea was not valuable enough. Years later, it became obvious that there was a real need for her invention. Windshield wipers are now on every automobile sold today. In 2011, Anderson finally received the credit she deserved. She was inducted into the National Inventors Hall of Fame. This organization recognizes the work of inventors whose contributions have made a difference in the world.

Stories about inventions will always have the potential for myths to creep in. Other stories might continue to go untold. Giving proper credit to

Mary Anderson's Window Cleaning Device was the first to effectively clear windshields.

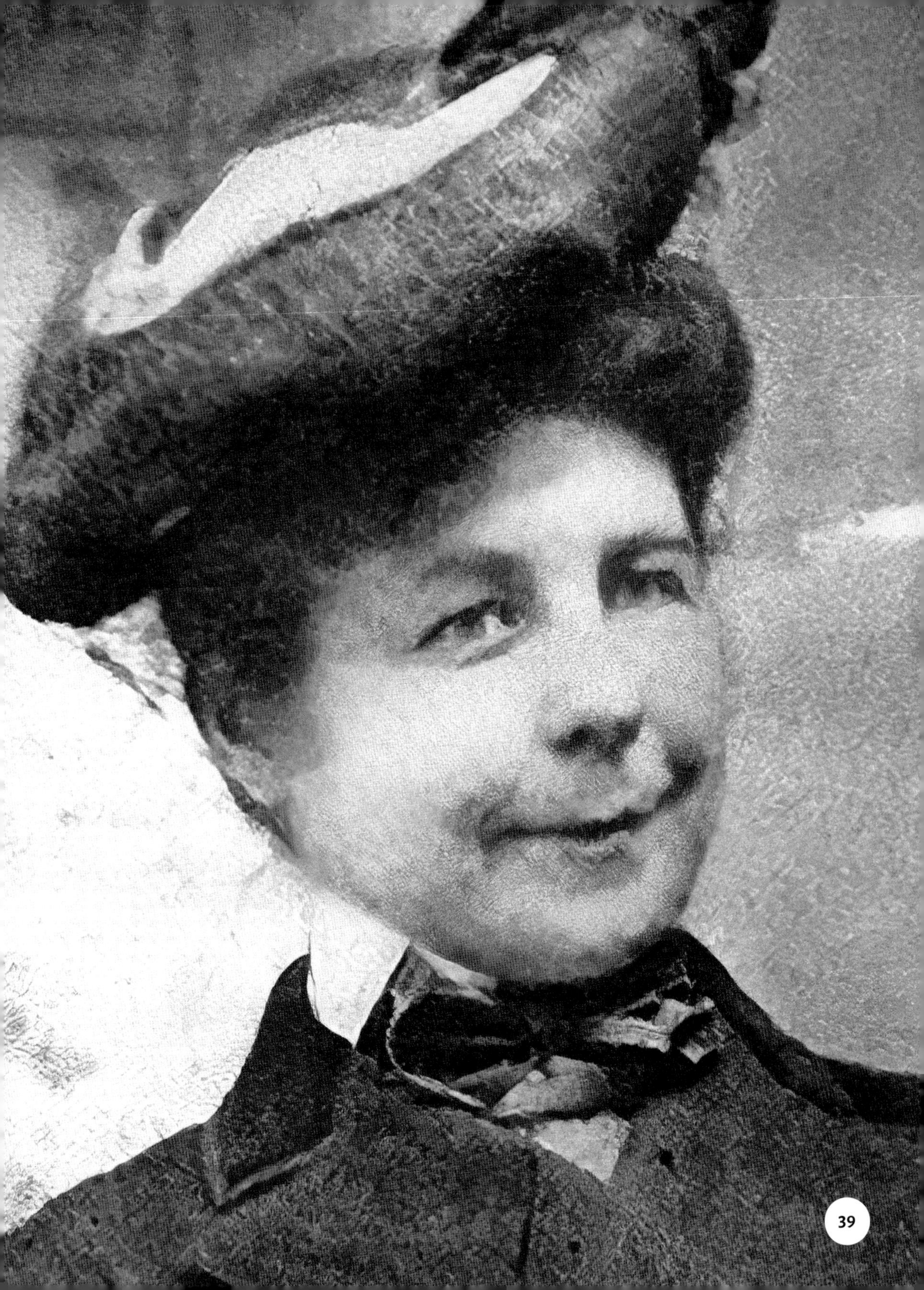

PERSPECTIVES
BECAUSE SHE WAS A WOMAN

Car companies finally realized the value of windshield wipers by the 1960s, after Mary Anderson's patent had expired. A male engineer named Robert Kearns stepped in to file his own patent for the invention in 1967. Sara-Scott Wingo is Anderson's great-great-niece. Wingo believes Anderson may have been overlooked because she was an independent woman. National Public Radio interviewed Wingo, who said, "She didn't have a father; she didn't have a husband, and she didn't have a son. And the world was kind of run by men back then."

each person who contributed to a particular invention can be challenging. But separating the facts from the myths is one of the best ways to honor inventors who may have been forgotten along the way.

STRAIGHT TO THE SOURCE

In 2017, professor Shontavia Johnson explained that enslaved Black inventors were overlooked in American history:

> Black inventors were major contributors during [the 1600s and 1700s]—even though most did not obtain any of the benefits associated with their inventions since they could not receive patent protection.
>
> Slave owners often took credit for their slaves' inventions. In one well-documented case, a black inventor named Ned invented an effective, innovative cotton scraper. His slave master, Oscar Stewart, attempted to patent the invention. Because Stewart was not the actual inventor, and because the actual inventor was born into slavery, the application was rejected.

Source: Shontavia Johnson. "With Patents or Without, Black Inventors Reshaped American History." *Smithsonian Magazine*, 16 Feb. 2017, smithsonianmag.com. Accessed 15 June 2020.

WHAT'S THE BIG IDEA?

Take a close look at this passage. What connections did Johnson make between being enslaved and being denied patents? How do you think Ned's invention would have fared at the patent office if he had been a white man at the time?

IMPORTANT DATES

1852
Elisha Otis invents the safety hoist, which leads to the popular use of elevators.

1868
Margaret Knight invents a machine that produces paper bags with flat bottoms.

1876
Alexander Graham Bell receives the patent for the telephone.

1879
Thomas Edison invents carbon filament, which improves the light bulb.

1897
John Lee Love patents his pencil sharpener. But he is overlooked because he is a Black inventor.

1903
The Wright brothers make the historic first flight. But some people believe the first flight actually belonged to Gustave Whitehead two years earlier.

1913
Henry Ford begins using the moving assembly line to mass-produce his automobiles.

1935
Parker Brothers makes a deal with Charles Darrow for Monopoly. Parker Brothers pays Elizabeth Magie only $500 for her Landlord's Game patent.

2011
Mary Anderson is inducted into the National Inventors Hall of Fame for inventing windshield wipers in 1903.

STOP AND
THINK

Surprise Me

Chapter Two discusses the invention of the elevator, the typewriter, and the telephone. After reading this book, what two or three facts about these inventions did you find most surprising? Write a few sentences about each fact. Why did you find each fact surprising?

Say What?

Studying inventions can mean learning a lot of new vocabulary. Find five words in this book you've never seen before. Use a dictionary to find out what they mean. Then write the meanings in your own words and use each word in a new sentence.

Take a Stand

Most inventions have many people contribute to them. But sometimes one person takes all the credit. Others who work on those inventions get overlooked or forgotten. Do you think it is important to give credit to everyone who works on an invention? Why or why not?

Dig Deeper

After reading this book, what questions do you still have about invention stories? With an adult's help, find a few reliable sources that can help you answer your questions. Write a paragraph about what you learned.

GLOSSARY

carbon
a chemical element that makes up minerals, plants, and animals

current
the flow of something in a certain direction

efficient
able to work well without wasting time or materials

entrepreneurship
creating and running a business

filament
a thin piece of material that conducts electricity and glows when heated

incandescent
giving off light when heated

internal combustion engine
an engine that burns fuel on the inside

mass-produced
made in large numbers using machinery

monopoly
a situation in which one person or company has complete control over products or services

patent
a legal right to make or sell a particular invention

ONLINE RESOURCES

To learn more about the facts and fiction of American invention, visit our free resource websites below.

Core Library CONNECTION
FREE! COMMON CORE MULTIMEDIA RESOURCES

Visit **abdocorelibrary.com** or scan this QR code for free Common Core resources for teachers and students, including vetted activities, multimedia, and booklinks, for deeper subject comprehension.

Booklinks NONFICTION NETWORK
FREE! ONLINE NONFICTION RESOURCES

Visit **abdobooklinks.com** or scan this QR code for free additional online weblinks for further learning. These links are routinely monitored and updated to provide the most current information available.

LEARN MORE

Hustad, Douglas. *Thomas Edison Invents the Light Bulb*. Abdo Publishing, 2016.

Thimmesh, Catherine. *Girls Think of Everything*. Houghton Mifflin, 2018.

INDEX

airplanes, 27–30
Anderson, Mary, 37–38, 40
automobiles, 8, 31–33, 37–38, 40

Bell, Alexander Graham, 17–19

Darrow, Charles, 5–6, 8

Edison, Thomas, 21–24, 25, 35
electricity, 22, 24–25
elevators, 13–14

Ford, Henry, 31, 33, 35

Gray, Elisha, 18–19

Knight, Margaret, 6

Lenoir, Étienne, 31
light bulb, 21–24, 25
Love, John Lee, 35–37

Magie, Elizabeth, 6–10

Otis, Elisha, 13–14

patents, 6, 14, 16, 18–19, 21, 36, 38, 40, 41

Sholes, Christopher Latham, 14–16

telephone, 17–19
Tesla, Nikola, 24–25
Tufts, Otis, 14
typewriter, 14–17, 19

Whitehead, Gustave, 28–30
Wright brothers, 27–30

About the Author

Tammy Gagne has written dozens of books for both adults and children. Her recent titles include *Fact and Fiction of American Colonization* and *Fact and Fiction of the American Revolution*. She lives in northern New England with her husband, her son, and a menagerie of pets.

no one person created an automobile completely on his or her own. The car was far too complicated for just one person to invent.

One reason Ford gets credit for inventing the automobile is that he perfected another invention that changed the world. That invention was the moving assembly line. This was an efficient arrangement of workers and machines in a factory. Each person in the line focused on one small part of the job. The assembly line made it possible to build a lot of automobiles in a short time. Ford began using the assembly line to mass-produce his automobiles in 1913. His cars were among the first to be sold to a large number of customers. Ford may not have invented the car. But he was the one to bring the invention to the public.

(No Model.)

J. L. LOVE.
PENCIL SHARPENER.

No. 594,114.   Patented Nov. 23, 1897.

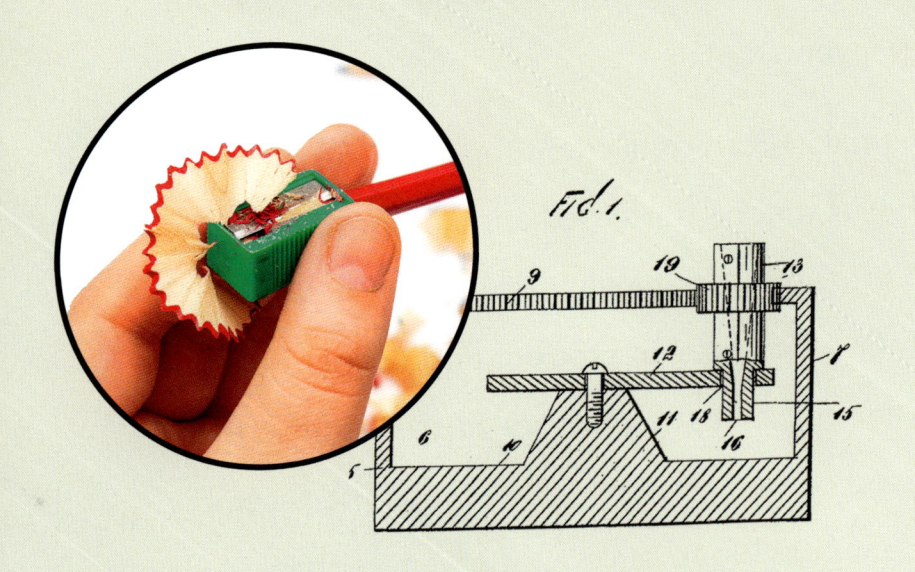

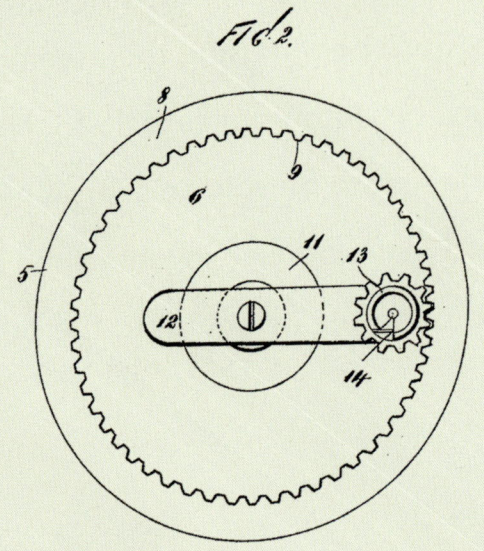

Fig. 1.

Fig. 2.

WITNESSES:
John Buckler,
C. Gerst

INVENTOR
John Lee Love
BY
Edgar Tate &
ATTORNEYS.

34